PEGASUS ENCYCLOPEDIA LIBRARY

Experiments and Activities
CHEMISTRY

Edited by: Aparna Chatterji
Managing editor: Tapasi De
Designed by: Vijesh Chahal and Anil Kumar
Illustrated by: Suman S. Roy, Tanoy Choudhury
Colouring done by: Vinay Kumar, Sonu, Kiran Kumari & Pradeep Kumar

CHEMISTRY

CONTENTS

Introduction	3
Wind dries things	4
Does it float or does it sink?	5
Liquid sandwich	6
Why is it easier to swim in salt water?	7
Boat powered by liquid soap	8
Sugar and soap move objects	9
Ice needs space	10
An ice which sinks	11
Indicators	12
Which ice is harder?	14
The properties of objects	15
Making stalactites at home	16
Plastic milk	17
Metal which swims on water	18
Which is lighter, alcohol or water?	19
A cloud in a bottle	20
The magic matchsticks	21
Changes in objects	22
The shooting cork	23
Making soap bubbles	24
A salt garden	25
Restoring the lustre of aluminum	26
Burning metal	27
Fire needs oxygen to burn	28
Heat and margarine	29
Salt melts ice	30
Soap vs Detergent	31
Index	32

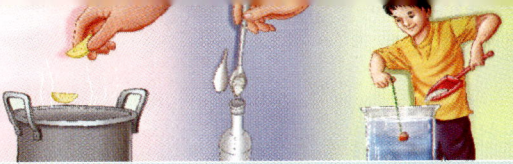

Introduction

Learning and experiencing new things is a continuous process. Children are much more inquisitive than we elders are. They are always bubbling with enthusiasm when it comes to knowing new things. That is the reason they are so full of questions. This enthusiasm should never be curbed; instead, it should be encouraged!

It is a proven fact that children learn the most by doing, experiencing and seeing things. Teaching them through books and worksheets only, does not suffice. We all know that 'seeing is believing'.

But sometimes due to the constraint of time and many other factors, elders are not successful in giving those experiences and exposure to their children which they deserve.

This encyclopedia on Chemistry which is termed as a 'natural science' will help the young readers to know more about the composition, structure and properties of matter as well as the changes it undergoes. They will also come to know about the chemical changes that take place in our everyday life like the combustion of fuel in our vehicles and common things like the melting of ice.

In other words, this encyclopedia will make the readers aware of the chemical changes that are going around in our lives and make them more comfortable with their surroundings.

CHEMISTRY

Wind dries things

The fact

The sun and the wind help wet things to dry which we will show in the following experiment.

What you need

Cotton cloth pieces approximately 50 by 50 cm and clothes-pegs.

How to do the experiment?

1. Soak all the cloth pieces in water, but don't wring them.

2. Hang them on clothes-lines in various spots—some in the shade where there's no wind, in the shade where its windy, in the sun where there's no wind and in the sun where its windy. You can also hang some to dry inside the house as well. Spread them out well.

What will happen?

The clothes hung in the windless and shady spots will take the longest to dry. Again, the one in the sunny and the windy spots will dry out the fastest. Stretching out the clothes properly also reduces the drying time.

Conclusion

The sun helps in the evaporation of water. Wind is also important in this process, because it helps to carry water molecules away from the surface of the cloth.

Does it float or does it sink?

The fact

Wood, Styrofoam and ice float on water regardless of their shape and size. But materials like plastic putty or metals may either float or sink depending on their shape, which we shall show in the following experiment.

How to do the experiment?

1. Put the marbles in the water and they will sink at once.
2. The same will happen with the plasticine lump.
3. Now take the marbles and the plasticine out of the water. Form a round, shallow pan out of the plasticine. Lower the plasticine pan into the water.

What you need

- A lump of plasticine
- Four glass marbles
- A vessel full of water

What will happen?

The plasticine will float.

A step further

Measure out several equal chunks of plastic putty. Organise plasticine boat sailing competition of who can make a boat which will take the biggest number of marbles without sinking?

Conclusion

For something to float, the amount of water that it displaces should weigh more than the object. The lump of plasticine sinks because of its shape which has low surface area. The amount of water that it displaces is very less. Thus, its own weight is more than the weight of the water that it displaces. This causes it to sink. But once you shape it into a boat, its surface area increases. This increases the amount of water that it displaces. Thus, the weight of the water that it displaces is more than its weight. Hence, the boat of plasticine floats.

CHEMISTRY

Liquid sandwich

The fact

Many liquids are similar to water and can be mixed with it easily. But there are also those which are very difficult to mix with water. One of them is oil.

What you need

- Water (coloured with some ink)
- Oil
- Glycerine
- A bottle with a stopper

How to do the experiment?

1. Pour equal quantities of oil and water into the bottle.
2. Close well and shake vigorously.

What will happen?

The liquids will appear to mix, but not for long. Soon the oil will be floating on top of the water.

A step further

Try adding another liquid to water. Pour in the densest liquid first, for example glycerine and then water.

Conclusion

Oil and water refuse to mix because their chemical natures vary. Oil is made of long hydrocarbons which are nonpolar. Water on the other hand is a polar molecule. Hence, oil does not mix in water. It is lighter than water; so it floats on top of water.

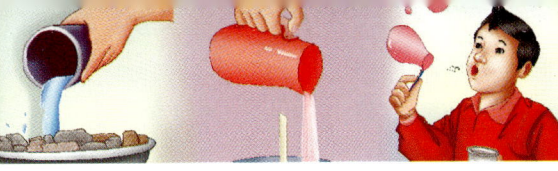

Why is it easier to swim in salt water?

The fact

We know that denser or heavier the liquid, the better things can float on top of it. Have you heard of the Dead Sea? Its density is the result of a very high content of salt. In the Dead Sea, you don't need to keep swimming to keep yourself on the surface. The following experiment will show you that it is easier to float in a denser liquid.

What you need

- A drinking straw
- Plasticine
- Container with ordinary water

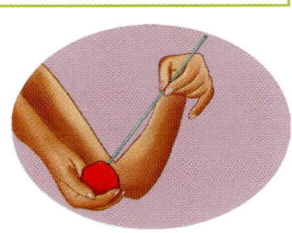

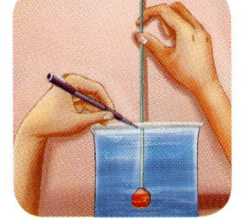  

- Container with salty water

How to do the experiment?

1. Fix a plasticine ball at one end of a drinking straw.
2. Lower the straw into a vessel with ordinary water until it floats upright.
3. Mark the water level on the straw.
4. Now do the same in a vessel filled with salty water.

What will happen?

The straw will sink deeper in fresh water.

A step further

Pour some more salt into the vessel full of water and repeat the experiment. Do you see any change?

Conclusion

The particles in a denser liquid are bigger or closer to one another than those of less dense liquids. Denser liquids exert more pressure on the objects on their surface. In the case of the Dead Sea, the very salty (very dense also) water exerts pressure on swimmers preventing them from sinking.

CHEMISTRY

Boat powered by liquid soap

The fact

Oil when mixed with water weakens surface tension

What you need

- A clean tub filled with water
- Greased paper
- Some liquid soap
- A ruler
- Scissors
- A pencil

How to do the experiment?

1. Draw an equal-sided triangle on the paper with a base of about 4 to 5 cm and a height of 8 to 9 cm.
2. Cut out the triangle and place it on the surface of the water.
3. Put a drop of liquid soap on your fingertip.
4. Immerse the fingertip into the water behind the triangle's base.

What will happen?

The paper boat will move.

  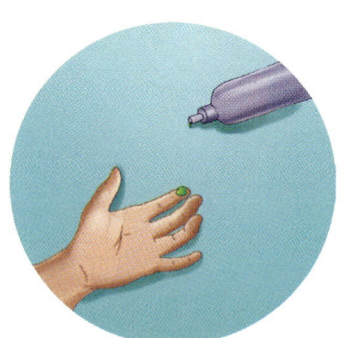 

Conclusion

The force between molecules on the surface of the water is bigger than that inside the vessel, forming surface tension. The surface of the water acts as a tight membrane. As the soap dissolves, it emits oil residues into the water. These residues weaken the surface tension and push the boat away from the spot where your finger touches the water.

Sugar and soap move objects

The fact

Soap can 'force' objects to move on the surface of water. Sugar can do the same, but the movement is different. Let's check.

What you need

- A bowl of water
- Matchsticks
- A sugar cube and a piece of soap

How to do the experiment?

1. Break the matchsticks into smaller pieces and allow them to float on the water.
2. Put the sugar cube into the centre of the bowl.
3. Now put the piece of soap into the centre of the bowl.

What will happen?

The sugar will move the pieces of wood towards the centre. And the soap will move the pieces away from the centre.

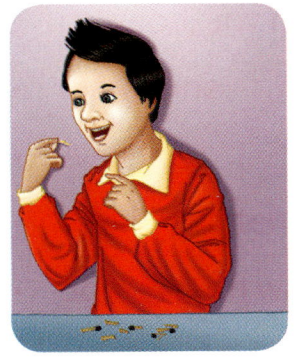   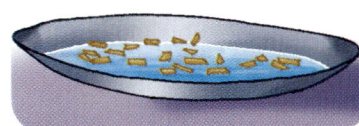

Conclusion

Sugar is porous and draws water into itself, pulling the pieces of wood along in the current it creates.

The soap, on the other hand, dissolves in water and decreases the surface tension. This propels the pieces away from the centre of the bowl.

CHEMISTRY

Ice needs space

The fact

We know that when water is cooled sufficiently, it turns into a solid form called ice. When that happens, it occupies more space than it had taken when in a liquid state. Let's prove this.

What you need

- Water
- Aluminium foil
- A funnel
- A freezer
- A small glass bottle

How to do the experiment?

1. Using the funnel, fill the bottle with water completely.
2. Place a piece of foil on the top and put the bottle into the freezer.
3. Take out the bottle out of the freezer after several hours.

What will happen?

The ice will lift the foil, showing that the water has expanded as it froze.

Note: Be careful, as the bottle may crack during the experiment.

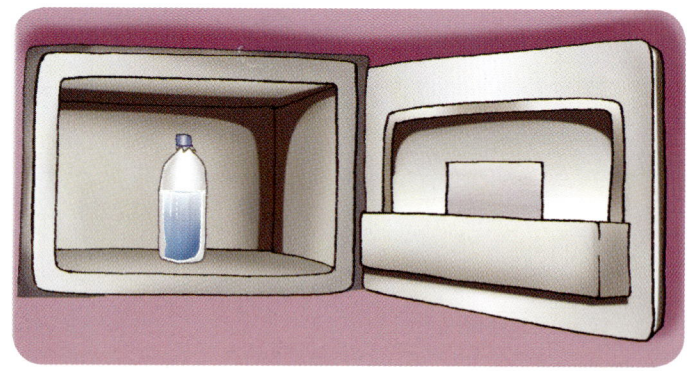

Conclusion

Most liquids get denser as they freeze, but in case of water, it is the opposite. When it turns into ice, it gets less dense and takes up more space. Ice floats on water because water is denser than ice. Icebergs float on the oceans for the same reason.

An ice which sinks

The fact

Many a time ice can sink in water even if only for a short while.

What you need

- An ice tray
- A freezer
- Water colours
- A plastic glass

How to do the experiment?

1. Pour some water into the plastic glass and mix some water colour in it.
2. Pour the coloured water into the ice tray and place it in the freezer. Let it freeze.
3. Pour some hot water into the plastic glass.
4. Put a cube of the coloured ice into the glass.

What will happen?

The cube will melt and the colour will spread through the hot water. The cube will also sink to the bottom of the glass, but after sometime it will once again rise to the surface.

Conclusion

As the ice cube melts, it turns into water. This melted ice is cooler than the warm water. Hence, it is denser. As a result, this freshly melted ice sinks. As it sinks, it is warmed by hot water and hence rises up again.

CHEMISTRY

Indicators

The fact

A surprising thing happens when you place pieces of red cabbage leaves in water. When you squish the pieces and water together, the water turns blue! If you add small amounts of different liquids, the cabbage-water will turn a variety of beautiful colours—pink, purple, teal or green. Try this activity to see some amazing colour changes.

What you need

- Red cabbage leaf
- Warm water
- Measuring spoons
- Measuring cups
- Plastic zip-closing bag
- 2 eye droppers
- 5 small cups (paper or plastic)
- Vinegar-teaspoon
- Laundry detergent-1 tablespoon
- 1 flat toothpick
- Masking tape
- Ball point pen

How to do the experiment?

1. First prepare the indicator solution.
2. Place the red cabbage leaf pieces into the zipped plastic bag. Add ¾ cup of warm water and close the bag tightly.

Indicators

3. Squeeze the bag of cabbage for a while and the water will turn dark blue. This dark blue liquid is your indicator solution.

Now you can begin your activity

- Using masking tape and pen, label the 5 cups as shown.
- Pour about 2 tablespoons of vinegar into the vinegar cup.
- Pour 2 tablespoons of water into the detergent solution cup. Add 1 teaspoon of detergent and swirl to mix.
- Pour 2 tablespoons of indicator solution into the three indicator cups.
- Use your dropper to put 1 drop of vinegar in the indicator + vinegar cup. Gently swirl the cup to mix. What do you observe?
- Use the second dropper to add 1 drop of detergent solution to the indicator + detergent cup. Gently swirl to mix. What do you observe?

Conclusion

Red cabbage-water is a special substance called an indicator. This means that when the colour of the cabbage-water changes, it says something about the liquid that was added to it. When the indicator is blue, it's considered to be neutral. Adding a neutral liquid like water will keep the indicator blue. You can make the indicator change to pink by adding an acid like vinegar, lemon juice or cream of tartar. The indicator will change to green by adding a base like laundry detergent or soap. Try adding different substances to red cabbage indicator and use the colour changes to classify each substance.

CHEMISTRY

Which ice is harder?

The fact

Sawdust makes ice harder. We will show this in the following experiment.

What you need

- Two round plastic containers (old butter or margarine cups)
- Sawdust
- Water

How to do the experiment?

1. Pour a little water into both cups.
2. Put some sawdust into one of them and make sure the water levels in both are equal.
3. Let both the cups freeze well in a freezer.
4. Now try to break the two ice disks.

What will happen?

The ice with the sawdust will be harder to break.

Conclusion

The sawdust acts as a reinforcement which makes the ice tougher.

The properties of objects

The fact

Every object has certain specified properties—hardness, colour, taste, smell, density, volume, inertia etc. Some of these properties change on their own, while we are able to alter others. It is easy to change the properties of cardboard and ice. The following experiments will show how.

fold the cardboard into an accordion shape; that is, make step folds in the cardboard.

What will happen?

In the latter case, the cardboard will hold up the glass.

What you need

- Three identical glass tumblers
- A piece of thin cardboard

How to do the experiment?

1. Place the two glasses apart and place the cardboard across them.
2. Place the third glass in the middle of the cardboard.
3. Now repeat the experiment, but first

Conclusion

When the cardboard is folded, many more particles (molecules) participate in holding up the glass.

CHEMISTRY

Making stalactites at home

The fact

Rainwater dissolves some types of rocks. Sometimes water seeping into a cave leaves a solid residue behind as it flows. With time, this residue forms a stalactite, a pillar hanging from the cave's ceiling. Try and make a small stalactite which will look much like the original.

How to do the experiment?

1. Make a saturated mixture of Epson salts in a vessel with hot water.
2. Cool and fill the jars with the mixture.
3. Hang the paper clips from the ends of the pieces of yarn.
4. Let the clips hang into the water-salt solution in the two jars stretching the yarn between them.
5. Place the jars in a warm and safe spot and put the saucer underneath the yarn.

What you need

- Two small glass jars
- Water
- Epsom salts
- Two paper clips
- Wool yarn
- A saucer

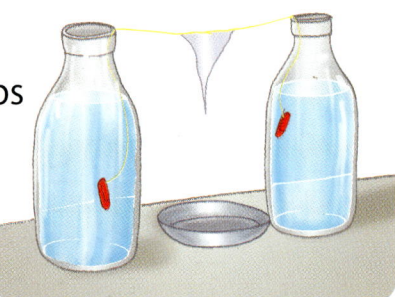

What will happen?

Over the following days, a stalactite will slowly grow from the yarn between the jars!

Note: Instead of Epson salts you can also use alum or sugar

Conclusion

The saturated solution soaks the yarn and slowly spreads through it. Some of it drips from the yarn. As it does, the water evaporates and leaves behind a salty residue.

Plastic milk

The fact

Some materials can be changed into different forms (other than their original) in which they remain. We call them 'plastic' materials. Wet clay, for example, is a plastic material, because it will retain any shape you give it. In this experiment, you will see that milk can also be transformed into a plastic material.

How to do the experiment?

1. Heat some milk in the saucepan.
2. When it begins to boil, slowly stir in a little vinegar.
3. Keep stirring. In a few seconds, the milk coagulates and becomes somewhat like rubber floating on water.
4. Let this cool. Then wash the coagulated milk with cold water and examine the 'plastic' material you have produced.

What will happen?

Vinegar is an acid. When added to hot milk, it causes a chemical reaction re-ordering the milk particles.

What you need

- A saucepan
- Milk
- Vinegar

Conclusion

The milk separates into a liquid and a solid plastic like lump. This solid is made of fat, minerals and a protein called casein.

CHEMISTRY

Metal which swims on water

The fact

Surface tension of water counteracts with the force of gravity and prevents metals from sinking in water. Due to surface tension, the surface of water acts like a stretched membrane.

What you need

- A vessel with water
- blotting paper
- a razor blade
- a metal paper clip
- a needle
- a fork

How to do the experiment?

1. Put the paper clip on a piece of blotting paper and place the paper on a fork.
2. Slowly lower the paper onto the surface of the water.

What will happen?

The paper will soon soak up water and sink but the paper clip will float.

A step further

You can do the same with a razor, a blade and a needle, and the result will be the same.

Conclusion

Metal is heavier than water and should sink. But the surface tension of the water is enough to counteract the force of gravity pulling down on the metal object preventing it from sinking.

Which is lighter, alcohol or water?

The fact

Alcohol is lighter than water. We can check this without weighing the two liquids through the experiment given below.

What you need

- Two identical small glasses
- An ordinary postcard
- Some water and some brandy

How to do the experiment?

1. Fill both glasses to the brim, one with brandy and the other with water.
2. Put the postcard on top of the water, lift the glass and turn it upside-down.
3. Place the water glass on the brandy glass and pull the postcard towards you a bit.

What will happen?

After a few minutes, the brandy will flow up into the upper glass and the water will sink to replace it.

Conclusion

Alcohol is lighter than water. When the liquids flow in the opposite directions, there is a little mixing too.

CHEMISTRY

A cloud in a bottle

The fact

When water is heated it turns into vapour. This vapour cools and condenses when it meets cooler air or a cooler object turning into tiny droplets of water which forms the cloud.

What will happen?

Clouds will appear in the bottle!

What you need

- A wide-necked glass bottle
- A piece of cardboard with a wide hole
- A few icecubes
- Warm water

How to do the experiment?

1. Pour some warm water into the bottle.
2. Place the cardboard over the top with the icecubes on it.

Conclusion

Water vapour which rises from the warm water, reaches the ice and is condensed as a cloud. The same happens in nature.

Water vapour rises to the cool upper atmosphere and forms clouds. Window panes are fogged in a similar manner when warm and moist air comes in contact with cold glass.

The magic matchsticks

The fact

Liquids have a tendency to rise in narrow tubes or are drawn into small openings. It is a result of the intermolecular attraction within the liquid and the solid materials. This tendency is known as Capillary action. The experiments given below will prove just this.

What you need

- A bottle
- A candle
- A cork stopper
- A pin
- A box of matches
- Water

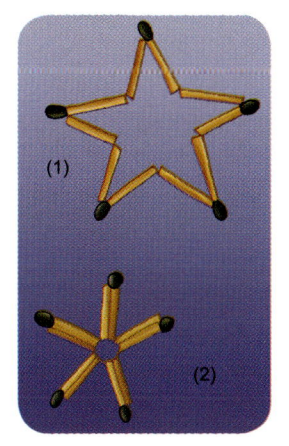

How to do the experiment?

1. Bend a matchstick so that the two halves form a right angle.
2. Pin it to the cork as shown.
3. Bring a burning candle near the match.
4. Pour some drops of water on the bended part of the match.

What will happen?

The match will straighten and burst into flame.

A step further

- Bend matchsticks into half. Place them on a plate as shown in picture 1. Drip some water on the bends. After sometime you will get a new arrangement, as shown in Picture 2.

Conclusion

The matchstick soaks up the water in tiny capillaries which causes it to straighten and come in contact with the flame.

CHEMISTRY

Changes in objects

The fact

Many a time relatively small changes done to objects can cause them to change their behaviour and assume new properties.

What you need

- A wide-necked bottle
- A hard-boiled egg
- A piece of paper
- A match box

How to do the experiment?

1. Shell the egg.
2. Put the paper into the bottle.
3. Throw in a burning match to set the paper on fire.
4. When the flames are the highest, close the opening with the boiled egg.
5. Wait for the fire to go out and the air in the bottle to cool.

What will happen?

The egg will slowly slide down into the bottle and then suddenly pop in with a bang.

A step further

You may use a banana skin instead of the egg.

Conclusion

The egg is driven down by the atmospheric pressure, which is greater outside than the thin air inside the bottle.

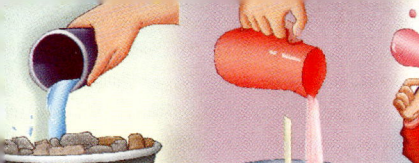

The shooting cork

The fact

Sodium Bicarbonate (baking soda) is a base which reacts with the acetic acid in the vinegar to produce water and Sodium Acetate. In the process, it also gives out carbon dioxide as a product. In this experiment we will show this.

What you need

- A bottle with a cork stopper
- Vinegar
- Bicarbonate of soda
- A table spoon
- Water

How to do the experiment?

1. Pour two tablespoonfuls of bicarbonate of soda into the bottle.
2. Wet the cork with water.
3. Pour two tablespoonfuls of vinegar into the bottle and plug it quickly with the cork (not too firmly).

What will happen?

The mixture will begin to hiss and bubble and very soon the cork will shoot out of the bottle.

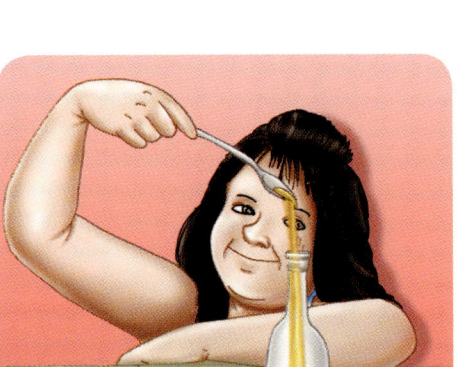
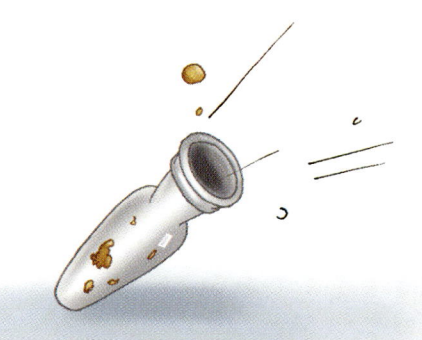

Conclusion

The cork will be expelled by the pressure of the carbon-dioxide formed in the reaction.

CHEMISTRY

Making soap bubbles

We all have been fascinated by bubbles made from soap water in our childhood. Let us make this soap solution and see whether we can still make soap bubbles or not.

What you need

- Water
- Detergent soap
- Glycerine
- A suitable vessel
- A grater
- A piece of linen

How to do the experiment?

1. Grate some soap in a container.
2. Dissolve it in warm water (the solution should be as thick as possible).
3. Strain the solution through the cloth.
4. Mix this solution with glycerine (three parts solution and two parts glycerine).
5. Let it stand for a while and then remove the white coating that will form on the surface.

How to use the solution?

Make loops out of wire, dip them in the liquid and blow bubbles in the air.

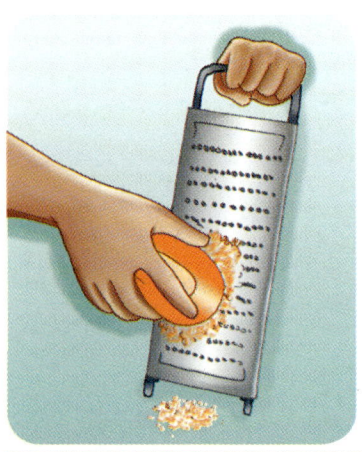  

Conclusion

When you blow into the mixture of water and soap, you add the air that forms the centre of the bubble. Bubbles burst when they dry out. Adding glycerine slows down the evaporation of water that causes the drying out. Hence, glycerine increases the life of the bubble.

A salt garden

The fact

Liquids have a tendency to rise in narrow tubes and are drawn into small openings. It is the result of the intermolecular attraction within the liquid and the solid materials. This tendency is known as Capillary action. The experiment given below will prove just this.

What you need

- A plate
- Warm water
- Table salt
- Vinegar
- Several porous rocks or pieces of coal

How to do the experiment?

1. Put the stones on the plate.
2. Dissolve the salt in warm water to the maximum possible density.
3. Add a tablespoonful of vinegar to the solution.
4. Pour the solution over the stones.

What will happen?

Several days later the salt will begin to 'grow' and cover the stones with beautiful crystals.

Conclusion

Due to capillary action, the salt water makes its way into the rocks and gradually evaporates leaving behind salt formations. The role of the vinegar is to eliminate greasy spots on the stones which obstruct the flow of the water.

Restoring the lustre of aluminum

The fact

Aluminium pots and pans get tarnished (turn dark) when they are not used for a while. They can be cleaned effectively with pieces of lemon. This is proved through an experiment given below.

What you need

- A tarnished aluminium utensil
- Lemon slices
- Water

How to do the experiment?

1. Pour water into the utensil and warm it on fire.
2. Once the water begins to boil, throw in the lemon slices.

What will happen?

The utensil's colour will become lighter.

Conclusion

The acid in the lemon reacts with the tarnish to form an aluminium salt which is easily soluble in water.

Burning metal

The fact

Metals have characteristic and well-known properties. They are good conductors of heat and electricity, they are malleable, they have lustre etc. Some metals have special properties.

How to do the experiment?

1. Light the candle.
2. Pour the powder slowly with the spoon on to the flame.

What will happen?

The aluminium burns easily and sparkles are formed.

What you need

- Aluminium powder
- A candle
- Match sticks and a spoon

Conclusion

This experiment proves that aluminium does have special properties.

27

Fire needs oxygen to burn

The fact

Fire cannot burn without oxygen. If we seal a burning candle in a glass jar, it will go out after it has used up all the oxygen. Oxygen makes up about one-fifth of the volume of air. We shall prove it with this experiment.

What you need

- A candle
- Plasticine
- A small saucer
- Food colour
- Coins
- A glass jar
- Water

How to do the experiment?

1. Fix the candle vertically on a lump of plasticine in the middle of the saucer.
2. Place four stacks of coins around the candle to form a base for the jar.
3. Pour coloured water (coloured with the food dye) into the saucer to the brim.
4. Ask an adult to light the candle and to place the jar carefully over it.

What will happen?

After a few minutes, the candle will go out and the level of water will rise.

A step further

Compare the duration of burning of different candles in different-sized jars. If they burn longer, then there was more oxygen in the jar.

Conclusion

The flame consumes the oxygen in the jar. As it is consumed, water enters the jar in place of the oxygen. The level of water will reach about one-fifth of the jar. The flame will go out as all the oxygen is consumed.

Heat and margarine

The fact

Stir hot tea with a metal spoon and soon you will feel the spoon getting hot from the tea. This is because the heat has travelled along the spoon from its hot end to its cool end. This kind of heat transfer is called conduction. This experiment will show how this happens.

What you need

- Three identically sized sticks made out of wood, any metal and plastic
- Margarine
- A knife
- A kitchen utensil (pot or pan)
- Some warm water

How to do the experiment?

1. Cut out pieces of margarine of equal size.
2. Place them on the end of the three sticks.
3. Put the sticks into the vessel as shown.
4. Pour warm water into the vessel.

What will happen?

The margarine on the metal stick will melt quickly, while that on the other two hardly melts at all.

A step further

Place pieces of chocolate along a spike and heat one end with a candle flame. The heat conducted through the metal melts the pieces one by one. You will soon see that you will not be able to hold the spike without using a cork stopper at the end as the end will turn very hot.

Conclusion

Metals are good conduct of heat, while wood and plastic are poor conductors of heat.

CHEMISTRY

Salt melts ice

The fact

Salt helps to melt ice. The following experiment will show this.

What will happen?

The ice around the string will begin to melt, but soon it will re-freeze together with the string. Now pick up the ends of the string and lift the ice-cube out of the glass.

What you need

- A glass of water
- An ice-cube
- Some thin string
- Salt

How to do the experiment?

1. Put the ice in the water.
2. Moisten the string and let it lie across the ice-cube.
3. Sprinkle a little salt across the string and the exposed side of the ice.

Conclusion

Salt causes the ice to melt. In this process, the ice loses heat but the cold ice-cube soon causes the salty water to freeze, whereby the string is trapped inside the ice. For this reason if there is ice on the roads in winter, a lot of salt needs to be used in order to make sure that all the ice is melted.

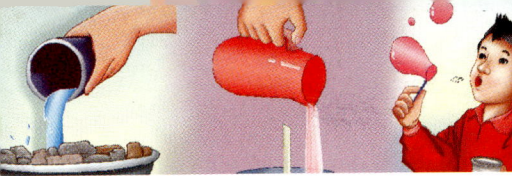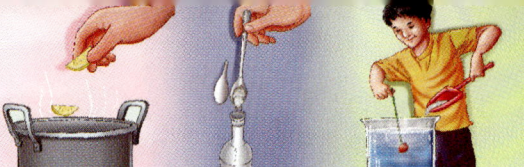

Soap vs detergent

The fact

Soaps do not lather well with hard water while detergents do. The following experiment will show us how.

What you need

- Measuring spoons
- Epsom salts
- Measuring cup
- Water
- 1/4 teaspoon of grated soap
- Any detergent
- Two glasses

How to do the experiment?

1. Dissolve 1 tablespoon of Epson salts in 2 cups of water. This makes "hard" water.
2. Put 5 tablespoons of "hard" water in each of the glasses.
3. Put 1/4 teaspoon of grated soap in one glass and label it 'soap'.
4. Put 1/4 teaspoon of detergent in the second glass and label it 'detergent'.
5. Cover the top of the glass with the palm of your hand and shake twenty times.

What will happen?

You should see a marked difference between the amount of foam produced by the detergent and the amount produced by soap. The detergent will produce more foam as compared to the soap.

Conclusion

Detergents are not affected by the presence of minerals in hard water while soaps do not foam well with hard water.

Index

A
alcohol 19

B
Bicarbonate of soda 23

C
capillary 21, 25
casein 17
conduction 29
cream of tartar 13

D
density 7, 15, 25

E
Epson salts 16, 31
evaporation 4, 24

G
glycerine 6, 24

H
hydrocarbons 6

I
indicator 12, 13
inertia 15
intermolecular attraction 21, 25

M
membrane 8, 18
molecules 4, 8, 15

N
neutral 13

P
porous 9, 25

R
reinforcement 14
residues 8

S
saturated solution 16
Sodium Acetate 23
stalactite 16
styrofoam 5
surface tension 8, 9, 18

T
tarnish 26

V
vinegar 12, 13, 17, 23, 25